MARS BEING RED

DATE DUE

MAY 1 9 2009	
MAY 2 6 2009	
MAR 2 2 2014	

DEMCO, INC. 38-2931

OTHER BOOKS BY MARVIN BELL

Rampant [2004]
Nightworks: Poems 1962-2000 [2000]
Poetry for a Midsummer's Night [1998]
Wednesday: Selected Poems 1966-1997 [1998, Europe]
Ardor: The Book of the Dead Man, Vol. 2 [1997]
The Book of the Dead Man [1994]
A Marvin Bell Reader: Selected Poetry and Prose [1994]
Iris of Creation [1990]
New and Selected Poems [1987]
*Drawn by Stones, by Earth, by Things That Have Been
    in the Fire* [1984]
Old Snow Just Melting: Essays and Interviews [1983]
*Segues: A Correspondence in Poetry (with William
    Stafford)* [1983]
These Green-Going-to-Yellow [1981]
Stars Which See, Stars Which Do Not See [1977]
Residue of Song [1974]
The Escape into You [1971]
A Probable Volume of Dreams [1969]
Things We Dreamt We Died For [1966]

MARS BEING RED

Marvin Bell

COPPER CANYON PRESS
PORT TOWNSEND, WASHINGTON

Cover art: Michael Spafford, *One Greek, One Trojan #15*, 2005. Oil on paper, 30 x 40 inches.

Copper Canyon Press is in residence at Fort Worden State Park in Port Townsend, Washington, under the auspices of Centrum. Centrum is a gathering place for artists and creative thinkers from around the world, students of all ages and backgrounds, and audiences seeking extraordinary cultural enrichment.

LIBRARY OF CONGRESS CATALOGING-IN-PUBLICATION DATA
Bell, Marvin, 1937–
    Mars being red / Marvin Bell.
        p. cm.
ISBN 978-1-55659-257-7 (pbk. : alk. paper)
I. Title.
PS3552.E52M37 2007
811'.54—dc22
2006101743

98765432 FIRST PRINTING

COPPER CANYON PRESS
Post Office Box 271
Port Townsend, Washington 98368
www.coppercanyonpress.org

Acknowledgments

Grateful acknowledgment is made to the editors who
published these poems, a few in earlier versions:

American Poetry Review: "Assisted Living Quarters,"
  "Cable News Night," "The Campus in Wartime,"
  "Doo-Wop," "Fifteen Minutes," "I Didn't Sleep," and
  "Slice of Life."
Asheville Poetry Review: "Regardless."
The Best American Poetry 2007, Scribner: "The
  Method."
Born Magazine (zine): "'Why Do You Stay Up So Late?'"
Caffeine Destiny (zine): "Poem Post–9/11/01."
*Chance of a Ghost: An Anthology of Contemporary
  Ghost Poems,* Helicon Nine Editions: "The Book of
  the Dead Man (Ghosts)."
The Chickasaw Plum: Politics and the Arts (zine):
  "Bagram, Afghanistan, 2002."
Chimera Review (zine): "The Broken Rose."
Coe Review: "Weapons of Mass Destruction."
Crazyhorse: "Days of Superman," "Dream of a Dream,"
  and "The Method."
Denver Quarterly: "Art in Wartime," "CQ," and "Elegy
  for Jim Simmerman, with a Call to Michael Burkard."
Empyrean Press (broadside): "I Didn't Sleep."
The Georgia Review: "Five to Seven" and "Why."
The Gettysburg Review: "The Book of the Dead Man
  (Memory)," "Veterans of the Seventies," and "What
  Things Are."

Hunger Mountain: "The Book of the Dead Man
(Writing the Dead Man Poem)."

The Iowa Review: "Astronomers May Have Reason for
Milky Way's 'Lumpiness,'" "Coffee," "Ode to Night,"
and "*Poseur.*"

Kenyon Review: "An Apology to the Vietnamese and
Iraqis," "Art Shoes," and "Bus Stop Essay on
Rampant Capitalism."

Long Journey: Pacific Northwest Poets, Oregon State
University Press: "People Walking in Fog" and "'Why
Do You Stay Up So Late?'"

The Long-Islander: "About His Eyes."

Lost Horse Press (broadside): "Coffee."

Natural Bridge: "The Book of the Dead Man (Recent
Dreams)."

Near East Review: "Archaic Apollo," "The Broken
Rose," "Her Shyness," and "Stupid Time."

The New Yorker: "Bagram, Afghanistan, 2002,"
"Homeland Security," "Oppression," and "Prodigal?"

Oregon Literary Review (zine): "It."

Paterson Literary Review: "Unable to Sleep in Frost's
Bed in Franconia."

Ploughshares: "Mars Being Red" and "People Walking in
Fog."

Poetry East: "Yes."

Poetry Miscellany: "Mirror Image" and "The Time I
Tore My Kneecaps Off (*La La*)."

Prairie Schooner: "Geezers" and "The Poems I Want to
Hear."

Rattle: "Deadline."

Salmon: A Journey in Poetry, Salmon Publishing (Ireland): "Theory of Relativity (Political)" and "'Why Do You Stay Up So Late?'"

Shakespeare's Wages, Gendun Editions: "The Broken Rose," "Poem Post–9/11/01," *"Poseur,"* and "'Why Do You Stay Up So Late?'"

Silk Road: "West Coast Oceanic."

Solo Café 2: "American Winter 2006" and "Bent."

The Southern Review: "The Book of the Dead Man (Time)," "First-Generation American, Now the News," and "Ordinary."

The Spoken Word Revolution Redux, Sourcebooks: "Bagram, Afghanistan, 2002."

Third Coast: "Stubby Sag Harbor Sonnet."

Visiting Frost, University of Iowa Press: "Unable to Sleep in Frost's Bed in Franconia."

Wednesday, Salmon Publishing (Ireland): "Theory of Relativity (Political)."

Willow Springs: "Hard Times for Army Recruiters" and "Messy."

CONTENTS

Dorothy

MARS BEING RED

Prodigal?

If I put some straw into the suitcase,
I'll always have a bed. Scraps of olive wood,
slow to light, dense, will burn all night.
Some hard pumpernickel for good gums.
A sad bundle of underwear. A leaf
dropped by a poor scrub oak to remind me.
It will be a long Monday when I go.
The alarm throbs inside me, the early news
is crowded with bodies returning.
I'm off to the front lines in the war to preserve
the privilege of myth-making,
the consternations of art, the nerve to think
the future and remember the past. Others
left their homes to sail and trek, to consort
with consorts and outsiders and so
learn the reaches of mankind's instinct
for survival. They breathed the fumes and ate
the stew. They lived among the heroic
who did not want another life, and if
they erred in creating bigger-than-life characters,
they broke bread with the unspeakable,
and that is worth something.

I Didn't Sleep

I didn't sleep in the light. I couldn't sleep
in the dark. I didn't sleep at night. I was awake
all day. I didn't sleep in the leaves or between
the pages. I tried but couldn't sleep
with my eyes open. I couldn't sleep indoors
or out under the stars. I couldn't sleep where
there were flowers. Insects kept me up. Shadows
shook me out of my doziness. I was trying hard.
It was horrible. I knew why I couldn't sleep.
Knowing I couldn't sleep made it harder to try.
I thought maybe I could sleep after the war
or catch a nap after the next election. It was
a terrible time in America. Many of us found
ourselves unable to sleep. The war went on.
The silence at home was deafening. So I
tried to talk myself to sleep by memorizing
the past, which had been full of sleepiness.
It didn't work. All over the world people
were being put to sleep. In every time zone.
I am busy not sleeping, obsessively one might say.
I resolve to sleep again when I have the time.

The Method

Of the knees we might say they beseech,
seen together on the floor, the head bowed,
wherefrom one senses penitence and dread.
From a future of the numerous, a single sword
is held aloft. It takes two hands. From the sound
of no-sound the soon-to-be-beheaded is aware
the steel blade is beginning to descend. At once
the stricken neck flowers, a thousand rosettes,
and the head, picked up by its hair, dripping,
is thrown thoughtless in the trash. For an instant,
if one could be measured, the mind must resist,
while in reality time stops. Something about it.
A kind of gumshoe diplomacy kicks into action,
asking for clear pictures it dare not show.

The Poems I Want to Hear

Poems in the spirit of those who know they will die.
In the swell of the horizon over land or over water.
In the exaltation of gulls but also crows.
In the bursting of the sun exhaling before the mirror of
    its body.
Also in the pull of the moon that moves tides above- and
    belowground.
On a path opposite the explainers.
After the fashion of scat singing, the blues, after the
    manner of symphonies.
And to each the form of its becoming as it becomes.
Ad-lib but knowingly, seat-of-the-pants with long cockpit
    experience.
Without the looking back of the classroom.
Without stopping short or running over.
Without prescriptions or diagnoses, with no compass, no
    north.
In the spirit of a circle.
That which is yet as straightforward and tautological as a
    lion or a rodent.
Nor in the jacket and handkerchief of good thoughts.
Nor bound to the waters of breathless sensation, nor the
    rock of relativist indifference.
Poems in the spirit of those who know they are dying.
Who have seen the soil blow away and return.

That a wind shall surface within us.

Those who live in the middle of the country know this
     can happen.

That the sun should enter a rock and remain there.

As occurs at noon in the Southwest when shadows are
     widest.

That the night should run to the north and there be
     re-candled.

Those in the Northwest of the country have walked in
     such light at midnight.

That plants should sweat and grasp at shape like any
     human being.

Southerners have heard the waters bubble with the
     breath of new life.

That men and livestock should shrink at a distance.

Westerners have felt the ground wrinkle and stiffen as it
     dries.

And the Coasts, there one looks abroad and is exposed by
     minus-tides.

That the life force should rise and fall.

We had driven to within fifty miles of the Arctic Circle
     when our tire shredded.

Fishtailing near the survival hut where one waits three
     days for the trooper.

A day of skating the tundra carries doubts of Earth's
     crust.

As one clear day at Haleakala shatters one's clock.

There is glacier time, tundra time, volcano time, what is
     time?

To believe in time is to clasp regret to one's bosom, is it
     not?

The Book of the Dead Man
(Writing the Dead Man Poem)

Live as if you were already dead.
Zen admonition

1. Writing the Dead Man Poem

When the dead man writes a poem, he immediately writes
    another one.
He writes another because two follows one.
So well does part two shadow part one that they cannot
    help but argue and marry.
He who would write a dead man poem must know that all
    things coalesce.
She who writes a dead woman poem must understand
    that perception is kaleidoscopic.
The dead man sees and hears every tangent, every
    approach, every blade of grass that bows this way
    then that.
When the dead man repeats himself, he never steps into
    the same line twice.
The dead man, after midnight, turns the key that coils his
    insides.
His poem lasts as long as his innermost spring remains
    compacted.
When the dead man's spring snaps outward and bites,
    then the poem has ended that defined the
    moment.
A dead man poem knows that the sentence is the key.
The sentence, sans enjambments, has redefined free
    verse.

Yet it is not the sentencing on the page alone but the
    sentence of time.
The dead man serves the sentence, he fluctuates between
    the long and short of it, between the finite and the
    infinite, between the millisecond and eternity.
Whosoever shall write a dead man poem must know in
    his bones that his lifetime is an event that splits
    another event in two.
That is why a dead man poem must have two parts.
You may think at any moment you are done with life—so
    many first thoughts, so many smarts, such agility—
    but you are not.
Later, you may think you had only begun at the finish, so
    complete was your escape from time while writing
    the dead man poem.
You may be discordant or discombobulated or delighted
    to feel the weight of a dead man poem.
For a dead man poem threads and disentangles, sews and
    slices, glues and fractures.
Its harmonies are made of missing notes and from words
    he would gladly take back.
It is in the dead man's mission to show up the illusions of
    time, the discrete, chaos, order, health, and
    whosoever misuses quantum mechanics one day
    and the death of armies the next.
Write a dead man poem if you must, but only if you must.
For the dead man hath no choice, he hath only blind luck
    and love.
He hath only his prophetic existentialism, his diary of the
    posthumous.

The true dead man book can be opened anywhere to the
fullness of life, what else was poetry ever for?

2. More About Writing the Dead Man Poem

It is also necessary to understand the abandonment of
distinctions.
To realize that a poem can be forbidding yet ephemeral,
while a dead man poem may run from side to side
or seesaw yet carry the gravity of the ancient.
Why this is so is of a matter embedded in mortality.
So deeply buried that vanity cannot mine it, it will take
poetry masquerading as prose, philosophy hiding
in the impulsive, the devil-take-the-hindsight,
shotgun-riding, seat-of-the-pants voice of the
very now without regard for itself to express the
consolations of time, and to say for once the
solace Jacob felt wrestling the angel.
Do I surprise you with my reference, very well then, I
surprise you.
I invite you now to write the dead man poem, the dead
woman poem, the poem of the dead chorus
fluttering the weeds with song.
For only then will you be one among the many, your
intentions subsumed in something larger than the
self.
Your sentences must be elastic, your thoughts flexible,
your heart given to the hidden acrobatics of dark
emotions.

That is all I can tell you.

To help you any more than this would be like the rain
   instructing a cloud—too late, too late.

The dead man is plugged in, he is the last vestiges of
   dead friends, he suffers the little children to grow
   up and away.

He hath lasted the lashing of night, he hath wrestled the
   angel to a draw.

Few will know how lasting his love.

For you cannot write a dead man poem if you have not
   known love.

Poseur

I confess what I did in the tombs and the displays, and
       how I filtered the reports through an hourglass.
I admit to turning out the green light in the grapes.
I own up to emptying the squid of its ink.
All because I conceived of a rope with a noose at the end
       of it.
And I imagined an alchemical tide smothering the shore
       in gold.

I am not even the corpse at the end of this idea.
I tried to refill the night, but my eyes were open.
The two ends of the equator unraveled as I tried to cross.
The peeled apple took its skin back before I could eat.

Stars swept up their rays and the Milky Way poured itself
       over the rim of the planet rather than be named
       on my maps.
I awoke and was dead, so I decided to take my own life,
       and ended up alive after my self-inflicted demise.

Coffee

The house smells of coffee, and I want some.
It's my coffee and I want it. I dreamt of coffee
and now I want it. I want the dream and the coffee
in the dream. It was my dream and my coffee.
Wait, no, it was *his* coffee in my dream. He wants
the coffee, and I want the coffee in my dream.
My god, it's my coffee, isn't it, and I want coffee,
that coffee, and *that* dream. The dream of coffee
is a wartime dream. This war is endless. I want
the war to end. I want to wake up and have it
be over. I want my coffee and my dream back.
It's his war and my coffee. Get out of my house,
Mr. President. You can get your own coffee.

Bagram, Afghanistan, 2002

The interrogation celebrated spikes and cuffs,
the inky blue that invades a blackened eye,
the eyeball that bulges like a radish,
that incarnadine only blood can create.
They asked the young taxi driver questions
he could not answer, and they beat his legs
until he could no longer kneel on their command.
They chained him by the wrists to the ceiling.
They may have admired the human form then,
stretched out, for the soldiers were also athletes
trained to shout in unison and be buddies.
By the time his legs had stiffened, a blood clot
was already tracing a vein into his heart.
They said he was dead when they cut him down,
but he was dead the day they arrested him.
Are they feeding the prisoners gravel now?
To make them skillful orators as they confess?
Here stands Demosthenes in the military court,
unable to form the words "my country." What
shall we do, we who are at war but are asked
to pretend we are not? Do we need another
naive apologist to crown us with clichés
that would turn the grass brown above a grave?
They called the carcass Mr. Dilawar. They
believed he was innocent. Their orders were
to step on the necks of the prisoners, to
break their will, to make them say something
in a sleep-deprived delirium of fractures,

rising to the occasion, or, like Mr. Dilawar, leaving his few possessions and his body.

Archaic Apollo

The man who invented Bigfoot said so
while people went on searching for the beast man
as once they trailed Apollo to find the sun
so they might relight its wick at dusk. Star parts
were the candelabrum of the gods,
and if we were squatters on a space boulder,
trespassers at the margins of life,
who among us had an inkling? It takes nerve
to smile and beget without a coating
of the fabulous. That there be more to a man
than the ripening in his loins, we have built up
the Abominable, the Loch Ness Monster,
crop circles and alien eyeballs too fast above
to be seen in their cockpits. The voices of
past centuries, hoarse from lack of water,
speak of lucent change, and a trailhead where
a god was spotted among magnetic lodes
of the Northwest. Of course the great Apollo
fell into disrepair and lives now in the mythic
remains of his statue, an absence fit for art.

Theory of Relativity (Political)

When I was young, dreaming of luminescent escapades set against the light of a great pearl hung in a sky that would otherwise be black, as if it were the one thing certain to survive the overwhelming forces of the tide of an invisible sea, I once thought of becoming a policeman but gave it up and became something else. Then one day the sea rose up and heaved itself from the sky, collapsing in exhaustion on the earth where it lay trying to catch its breath. From this I learned that the fiercest incandescence can be swallowed by accident if an open maw goes by, swimming or flying. From the cultivated moon we must shift our attention to a speck of sand hung in an eye from which tears have fallen onto the earth and lie sighing. If we are going to be the world's policemen, we had better train for microcosms and the faces of wristwatches, for the damage one does in a small area just by turning around can cause tremors that travel by root and branch and spread like cracks in the crust of the desert. I and my countrymen, being patriotic, listen for organic pressures building under the surface, and in any event one does not want to play God when God plays God.

Stupid Time

I have ten more minutes until 1 a.m.
I promised myself 1 a.m. but not a minute more.
Until 1, I swore to picture the victims of war.
It is ten more minutes before I can put down
this pencil. Ten minutes until a stupid time.
In ten minutes, I can relax in the shadows,
sink into the bed, draw up the covers,
and give the ghosts the bum's rush when they hoot
at my deadline. The dying overflow
the ground set aside for them, and broken vets
have claimed the sidewalks. The stoves are frozen
that used to warm families in peacetime.
The casualty numbers go into desk drawers.
And I see in my mind the soldier whistling
at the front under a thin blanket. And the one
standing guard like a monument off its pedestal.
I have ten minutes more, which is all I can stand.
I have to go on, while time runs backward.

American Winter 2006

Through the snow one makes out a word now and then,
enough to know that the distance between
light and dark has narrowed. The time it takes
to go to war has shrunk, and a missile
can fly a thousand miles at blinking speed.
Don't nobody say let's think about it.
Waiting is wrong now, hesitation has become the time
between almost and too late. Who among us
carries a lantern in case an honest man should appear?
We can keep the search going, I believe we can,
if we can breathe so deeply that the press is thrown
from our chest as we exhale, and if we can
hold our breath when we need to.

Cable News Night

An after-midnight siren rises from the street
to cut through the sound of the hotel heater
during a cold snap. The spirit is on the stair
that will soon possess us until morning, but
the twenty-four-hour news will be channeled
without splitting a seam or twisting a foot
since it no longer requires a messenger,
a yodeler, a smoke signal, a crier, a pigeon,
or an arrow bearing a note. Throw a stone
through a window and the law will sponge up
the footprints by the sill, trace the grain
of the getaway tires, and filter the trash
for a candy wrapper or soda can bearing
the DNA of the coward. Anonymity is passé.
The smell of paper files has been quarantined
in the part of the brain for nostalgia, where
an egg fries on a sidewalk, men tip their hats
and their hands, and the eyes are the windows
of the soul. If you want to know how it was,
make the siren sound into the shape of a man
or woman, picture their age and condition,
taste the painkiller aftertaste they wake to,
and breathe and breathe. Later, the name
will appear in the news, bypassed en route
to the battlefield, the stadium, the fashion runway.
We are such minds as have no mind to
linger, though we slow down at the scene.

Messy

Morning's old news from another time zone.
Another video, last night's big-eyed child
cradled by a weary soldier or firefighter
across battle lines and a shifting border.
Off the walkway to step around the water
where the shopkeeper is hosing the concrete,
the aspirate knocking of the stream, shaped
by contained pressure, ups the ante because
I have bet on consciousness to be awake
even as the sales of armament overtake
the shopkeeper and the street vendor, reduced
to cleaning the neighborhood underneath
the saw-sound of engines above the cloud cover.
Yes, it all goes together, it is messy. The story
of a child rescued from the destroyed city
for a better life omits the residue. I have inside me
the click of a single round squeezed off
in a sniper-scope war, and the tidal thudding
of wave after wave of bombers melting steel
and the puncturing whoosh of bunker missiles
and the painting of napalm and the spray of
cluster-bombing, which returns me between wars
to the ideal, the sublime, the transcendent,
the transformative and the aesthetic escapes
of the mind from a cracked and patched heart.
I am only seventy, think what it means to be
twenty and the sidewalk taking you past dry goods
and home appliances, past a pocket of cold

at the ice cream window, past the hissing espresso,
and at the far end the dark of the movie house
telling a story that never happened. I am my insides,
as you are, try to tell me the paycheck is bigger
than the hole in your gut where peace used to be.

What Things Are

A mallet is a tool. It can put you to sleep.
Ice is a mineral. It can put you to sleep.
A sponge is a lacing that can lull you
into the warmth of sleep. It's not hell.
String, who would think string, but then
they've been stringing them up for forever.
Rope is a lot of string. In the park, well,
that's a safe place where they find a body
once a week. You can pick up a packet
of information from the hive they call
"Social Services." They fought over salt
and land. They fought for sea-lanes.
They fought to be free to read any book
over the midnight oil, and they fought
for oil. I don't know what poetry is
in their hands, or who they are. When I
look to see, it comes up blackness.
If I listen, it's the cacophony of alarm
where there were rustling leaves
and crickets. The air tastes as if it
came from Congress after an all-nighter.
Who wants to inhale the underside of
all the beautiful city architecture?
You can smell the bacterial mud, the spit,
the phlegm, the bad food and camphor
of urban America. But you can't touch it.
It dissolves as you approach, the crowd

scatters to let the lucky ones through.
What you couldn't reach while alive
turns up in the parks, under the trestles,
down at the river and over the grates.
They are selling their kidneys. They offer
their bodies because they want to live.

Hard Times for Army Recruiters

It was late date night and the movie monster
stepping on the crushed buildings and bodies
roared in surround sound of ribs splintering
and ghastly expulsions of the greenish fluids
that accompany last meals. It was just a movie,
not a battlefield, not a radiated wasteland
from an n-plant meltdown, just a bebop chain
of speedy effects to encourage embracing
and a kiss or two. Romance is still the best
interruption during wartime and natural
catastrophe, and we care, too. Love is like
going to another world, and who today wishes
to quit grappling in the balconies of cinemas
just to enlist for the promise of military bearing
and a uniform some pretty girl will like.

The Campus in Wartime

Sweet corn sweetens the air by the gas station
as the Torah students hurry by to Hillel House,
the coatless short-skirted social butterflies
totter toward happy-hour double-drink specials,
the rabbi adjusts his tallis and the bartender
lines up the pints, half-pints and pitchers.
Three thousand of ours and thousands of theirs
are too many body bags to bury in the mind,
so while the gas of rotting bodies seeps up
from the ramshackle coffins and folded flags,
the young seek books or booze to soften the ache.
This year's few stalks of corn are one small
businessman's salute to the land. He may need
to fuel the air with toxic waste to earn a living,
but he has in mind the purity of original desire,
which some call sin but the half-Hasids know
as the life force, and the barflies toast. Let us study
the future, for it shall be the cradle of the past,
siring a blue abyss aflare in the lamp we call a sun.

Assisted Living Quarters

Wheelchairs colliding in the lobby
at dinner hour, the elderly rolling in from a brief
breath of fresh air as they were pushed
through the atrium to an elevator whose doors
slide slowly to let the chairs and walkers
in, and just in time—never to miss the social hour,
the health once-over and the all-you-can-eat
in two sittings. They take to their rooms
extra bread, tea bags, napkins. If no one
knows what's next, these aged know
they know. I can hear her breathing over
the walker, a lung-scraping where once
was a lightly rasping wind and before that
a breeze and before that an inaudible intaking
and expiration that involved no chest-raising
and collapse. The smokers are benched
beyond the door. Each person gets worse
in her own way. She who tottered on heels,
petite, positive in outlook, outliving four husbands,
finds only slippers fit now. It takes the morning
to prepare to go to lunch, what with making a fist
to make her fingers bend and reaching
high in the air to grab a little more time. All
the mothers have seventy-year-old babies.

The Book of the Dead Man (Memory)

1. About the Dead Man and Memory

If there had only been a window to the past.
If there had been a smear of belladonna, a hint of an
    alphabet in the smoke, a flame licking at the
    extraneous, a drum roll to announce the meaning.
The dead man poked his memory as if it were coals.
When he raked the embers, they sweat sparks.
If there had been a glass through which one could see
    behind oneself.
If the scissors had not marched inexorably down the
    seam.
He'd have been happy to scrape by, casting yarns of land
    and sea into the soapy foam that kept cleaning the
    shore.
If there had been a magic pill, a fire-walking epiphany, a
    panacea under the photographer's cloth.
Never mind, the dead man has made his getaway.
Like an umbrella wrenched by the wind, like an egg
    rolling downhill, like a wagon without brakes, like
    sirens that won't stop, the dead man is here and
    gone.
Where on the globe, where in the cradle of civilization,
    where in the garden of figs and exotic mosses, will
    he find the past?
The dead man rings up the millions who tried.
He gathers the bones and artifacts in baskets, he piles
    the buttons and buckles, the knives and numbers,
    the shoes and boots.

In a twist of fate, under a lilac sky, kin to mica and
      calcium, the dead man rests for a moment,
      considering.
He knows the latest, but he is not telling.

2. More About the Dead Man and Memory

By now there are dead man poems all over the earth.
Dead man and dead woman poems.
If there had never been Dadaism, Surrealism,
      Existentialism, the Absurd or the Prophetic, there
      would never have been a dead man poem.
If there had never been unreality.
If there had been no mind, no knowing that one knows.
If there had not been etymology, if the insects had not
      multiplied.
If there had been only the affections and affectations of
      the sublime, as the sun slid from arc to arc.
If there had never been a post–World War, there would
      have been no second dead man poem.
Now nostalgia regrets its big shoes and calloused
      footprints.
Now the backyards of nature are the gardens of a former
      world.
For it was dead man nature to separate, to carve out, to
      homestead and stake.
It was Dead Man and Dead Woman who came first.
If the water could not breathe, if the steam grew heavy
      with grit, if the cloud burst with particulates, if
      dew encrusted the grass, if eating an apple

became the mask of resistance, the dead man
could still pull up the blanket.
If there had been a floor that did not give way, a
philosophy that could sew a red thread
through stone, an underfoot that was glass.
For the dead man looks up and down as he kisses the
yellowing clusters of lilies that signal a
breaking fever.

Mirror Image

in memoriam, D.R.

Now I wonder if
in walking
into the sea up to his waist,
was he trying to kiss
his broken reflection? Did the first
wave buckle his legs,
and did an onlooker see his hand
appear to wave from a sliver
of foam? It was and is
a riddle, truncated
by his death. His penned valediction
did not scorch others, but bespoke
the whir of his mind, a scent of wet ash,
and the bitter saliva of one
in whom the hum of the universe
pressed to escape. He carried
a pocket book, *New World Writing.*

Elegy for Jim Simmerman, with a Call to Michael Burkard

It takes a long time to break up a book. The dark words,
the hard cover, the spine—they obstruct,
and you aren't strong enough to crack the syntax.
Where's the author? Maybe he knows how to bury
his books, the so-called immortals and his own
testament to anything. He has to be angry enough
to render the language in bellicose shreds. This has little
to do with Burkard in hiding or Simmerman
in the grave. Nothing at all to do with the fox light
across snow, or the boats that once grooved the waves
to find American names for the children.
It's always steerage where they prize a book
and reread it by dim light and puzzle out
the life someone must have lived to have such words.
When they landed in the New World, they held
the bruised book, the beloved, as a rabbi holds
a prayer book at a funeral. It had been winter. Now it
was summer, and there was no easy way to track
the fox and no call that could call it back.

Slice of Life

You take a window, a seat at the window,
and you look through the slats
of the half-open blinds because it's a slice of life
to be sitting without waiting. I'll be walking
on the shore when the tide claps a little,
breaking a wave into sea-shot that swarms over
the driftwood, and I'll turn my head to catch some of it,
and press the sand as I walk, looking for
the washed-up pieces of sea life and boat life,
and it will be a kind of end-of-days experience,
what with the source of life rolling in and out,
while you at your window watch for my return.

I could be walking along the shoreline,
edging downhill, my shoes covered now and my ankles
wrapped in heavy socks, and still
I veer farther out, knowing I cannot float or swim
but am old, terribly aware that I am now old,
and wishing to make an easy ending for you
but not knowing how. So I think what's possible,
the water at hand, the bridge above, the Sound ferry
that sometimes docks a passenger short.
Someone might have been at the rail, no one is sure.
And you sitting home by a window
will be expecting me, a fault in my facade, my plan.

I have outlived my insurance, but not my future.

People Walking in Fog

They try to watch themselves, drifting in a white sigh,
the boats and trees, and themselves, too,
when they think of it, spun from sheets of gauzy droplets
with which to tar the morning white and walk upon it.
The horizon yawns. The earth is liquid. They can feel
it, and not just it but the blanket meaning of it.
Here, bravado is the pretense of the immortal
before the infinite. There being no other side,
they must surrender to *this*, seeing they cannot
see far, find a door, hack a hole, or mark a spot.
Goats love fog. Parked lovers and beachcombers
love fog, and those who fear the authorities,
and the camera-shy love it, and they adore it
who wish to be wrapped in beauty so delicate
one must step outside it to be able to see it.

Mars Being Red

Being red is the color of a white sun where it lingers
on an arm. Color of time lost in sparks, of space lost
inside dance. Red of walks by the railroad in the flush
of youth, while our steps released the squeaks
of shoots reaching for the light. Scarlet of sin, crimson
of fresh blood, ruby and garnet of the jewel bed,
early sunshine, vestiges of the late sun as it turns
green and disappears. Be calm. Do not give in
to the rabid red throat of age. In a red world, imprint
the valentine and blush of romance for the dark.
It has come. You will not be this quick-to-redden
forever. You will be green again, again and again.

CQ

"From the French, sécurité (safety or, as intended here, pay attention). CQ still means, literally, 'attention' but in amateur radio its meaning is perhaps more accurately described by Thomas Raddall who compared it to yelling 'Hey, Mac!' down a drain pipe."

American Radio Relay League

I early liked the late-night static of ham radio,
the coded disruptions of dead air, the clicks of the key,
the metallic heat of the black, dimpled receiver chassis,
the toggle switches, the coils, the color-banded resistors,
the layered plates of the variable condenser, the plug-in
      crystals.
I liked, the way a boy likes, the amateurs themselves,
their radio shacks lit by dials and smelling of solder. They
were odd souls, of few words, preferring to transmit
a band of dots and dashes to a faraway ear,
and quickly moving on to the next, tapping away
the two-letter call that meant, "Is anyone out there?"

Homeland Security

Two owls have perched at the property line,
and a scraping on the porch means the postman
is wiping his shoes before continuing
across the yards, three homes' worth of catalogs
and ads, and the occasional letter, all cradled
in the crook of one elbow. I'll be getting an offer
of money, a map to riches, a new future
that has come out of the blue. Today I finger
each envelope before opening, and I admit
I feel for wires and beads of plastic explosive
amid the saliva. The daily rags speak
of a dirty bomb. The government tells me live
in a wooden house with a hurricane lamp,
a gas mask and flares, while it arms
an impervious underground temple from which
it can map the surface, choose a site
anywhere on the globe, and call down the rain.

Art in Wartime

In an age of explosives, we feel less
for the old war dead, now that it
happens around us, and faster. We are
inside, part of the circle, handing on
the plastic to the next person, coddling
the fuse before it is seated, as prideful to be
part of the concussive flaming to come as once
we felt enlarged by good deeds. That cell phone ring
cutting the baby's cry and the shrieks in the street
may be the signal to set the timer. Listen in. For it is
now, always now, at the decisive moment.
What music, food or fashion accompanies
this sleazy assault that tries to employ art
to devour the dead? The endless list of names
etches within us the splayed limbs, the grief,
the anger and ideals that mount at the edge
a data bank for cheap thrills, art apart.

Deadline

"Bodies left to rot in the bush char in the sun."
I have to pause the taped replay of the news
to catch my breath. It's taxing to keep abreast
of brush fires, abuse, disease and war,
and the late-night talk show funnymen mocking
villainy and genius equally to top the ratings.
How deep can our feelings go when the airwaves
rain bodies and the camera pans in focus
the urban homeless in a shower of fast film?
The newscasts are dust in vapors, and a map
where stickpins mark the travels of anchormen.
Art won't medicate the causes, the witty ennui,
or the downward spiral of dunces who cover
the brown air, the bombers aloft, and sometimes
hit a target before moving on. An army of forklifts
stands primed to carry out the morning headlines.
Today's evening news expires at midnight.

Fifteen Minutes

What can one do with fifteen minutes, of what use
is a reflex that runs its course but halfway,
a man who pushes a child in a swing and stands waiting
vainly for the swing to return, a man any man arriving
at the station in time for the train that no longer runs,
the names of depots now nonsense of nostalgia
without a period to stop at. So be it, says our philosopher,
whose own thoughts on time are disbelieving,
hence timeless. Wait by the tracks, by the firehouse,
by the train station or dance hall, wait, and events
will recur that only half-occurred the first time
since the moment allowed no retribution,
which is to say one who follows a bus out of town
will not catch it if it is only going one way.

Unable to Sleep in Frost's Bed in Franconia

The floor shone from nightmare.
It made little difference which path I took
chasing oblivion—mind's eye or the avenue out.
He, too, walked for hours just to meet up
with midnight. Who walks these long nights
has seen in the moon the cragged face of a farmer
lighting the withered crops that live but
a short season. And by rock walls that rose only
to clear a field, has listened hard to the voices
that blur the vision of one's time:
smear of tree sap and the juice of crushed fruit,
blood from the fly and the gorged spider. Thus it was
that I lay expecting something of the old man's
genealogy. I heard a cracking wise
in the floorboards, or so I thought, as I looked for sleep.
It was chilly. I had only a light blanket,
which I pulled over my head to hold my breath in.

Dream of a Dream

I dreamt about trying to remember,
but I couldn't. There must have been
a face in it, several faces, and shoes,
and there could have been a gravesite,
perhaps mixed feelings such as curiosity
and with it a lingering fear of the unknown.
I would tell you, if I could call it up again,
but it remains in the dark. Wake me
at 3 or 4 a.m. and I will mumble to you
my dreaming when the ringing began,
and I believe it will be the dream I had
that now and then returns, each time
with a face, but none I can remember.

Her Shyness

Shy is like, is like
what others are, or must be. *They* are shy,
or they would lift their eyes. And you
a powder puff of Pegasus if ever there were
among the blue toiletries
in the tiled desert of those preparations
you endured at the high noon of expectation. Oh, shy,
since you ask, is like the inside of a fishbowl:
look how big the eyes are,
and you the smallest in the tank,
if they only knew. You were happy enough not to see.
And is there anything harder
than to look at another, especially someone like yourself,
for whole minutes, closer than
through a microscope or telescope or one of those infra-red
gun sights, though of course with no bullets.
What are you like? When asked, it
touches the five points of every star in the sky.
Even to *think* of touching—somewhere there must be
a universe so sensitive
the marching of ants is heard in the concert hall.
The audience leans forward to listen. There,
the mule has feelings,
and the grackle, loud thief of all concerned,
is told to shut up
because, after all, hasn't he had enough?
Now include all animals in this made-up world—
from our second sight,

from our molecular rebirth—
and all brainless creatures,
all plasmatics. For the mule and the grackle
are but two on the vast field of the common.
I know we should care more.
But whom shall we care for,
whom shall we shy from? No, not entirely,
just here on Earth, in the clockwork.

Doo-Wop

He believes the tar pits hold bones but preserve
no emotions, and he believes space is matter.
He still thinks a kiss with full lips transformative,
the hope of a country boy with an uncultivated
heart, from the era of doo-wop and secret sex,
when the music was corny, clichéd and desperate
like teenage love. Who now will admit that poetry
got its start there, in the loneliness that made love
from a song on red wax, from falsetto nonsense.
Who does not know that time passing passes on
sadness? A splinter of a song lyric triggers shards
of memory and knots in his gut. He regrets he was
lashed to the mast when the sirens called. He
believes the sea is not what sank or what washes
up. There are nights the moon scares him.

Poem Post–9/11/01

Eastern Long Island

The air has been torn by helicopter blades.
The sky tries to heal itself but the rotors keep churning.
The late-night disc jockey sits in a hot spot spinning
       songs.
Exhausted gas falls from idling autos parked by the bay.
The stocks were up, as they say, "modestly."
This is the national news, supported by people like you.
I wake up with whoever is talking on the air.
I cannot see the rooftops or the basements that pepper
       their reports.
The attics of my neighbors lean with the weight of fading
       memories.
My totems, a polished piece of hematite.
A triangle of carved Chinese jade.
A medical necklace.
The basic moral questions.
For example, is a total commitment to the life force
       demonic?
For example, is ethics a luxury of circumstance?
For example, how thin is the ice?
Dark chocolate, they say, is the better for being
       bittersweet.
Try to see where you are, oppressed by the thumping of
       the copters.
A promise has been made to air an entire season of the
       mortuary show.

A man in a three-piece suit steps on the edge of a shovel
    to break ground for a community garden.
The tall Whalers Church standing stark white surrounds
    a resonant cavity.
You can picture the boats jostling the waves and the
    whale tail slapping.
When the harpoon hits, the exhalation shakes the tide,
    then the exaltation.
When disturbed, the otherwise free-flowing air terrifies,
    come nor'easters.
The disc jockey can't smooth it over when the helicopters
    come.
The parked lovers lose the moment.
The words from the front lines return to us chopped up.
We could have told one another before this din began.

"Why Do You Stay Up So Late?"

Late at night, I no longer speak for effect.
I speak the truth without the niceties.
I am hundreds of years old but do not know how many
    hundreds.
The person I was does not know me.
The young poets, with their reenactments of the senses,
    are asleep.
I am myself asleep at the outer reaches.
I have lain down in the snow without stepping outside.
I am frozen on the white page.
Then it happens, a spark somewhere, a light through
    the ice.
The snow melts, there appear fields threaded with grain.
The blue moon blue sky returns, that heralded night.
How earthly the convenience of time.
I am possible.
I have in me the last unanswered question.
Yes, there are walls, and water stains on the ceiling.
Yes, there is energy running through the wires.
And yes, I grow colder as I write of the sun rising.
This is not the story, the skin paling and a body folded
    over a table.
If I die here they will say I died writing.
Never mind the long day that now shrinks backward.
I crumple the light and toss it into the wastebasket.
I pull down the moon and place it in a drawer.
A bitter wind of new winter drags the dew eastward.
I dig in my heels.

The Broken Rose

Mozart fought with Beethoven, it was fierce.
And Mozart threw porcelain vases into the future,
hoping to score a hit, and he called Beethoven dirt
and dirty names such as only mothers recall,
names normally hidden under umbrellas
when people walk in the mud and mutter in the rain.
There was no stopping Mozart in his youth
because he had a perfect mind, and his hearing intact.
One day he decided that the oceans are asleep
when it comes to genius, and Mozart dared Time
to wake up further and to do it any better.

Time and the oceans snored, especially
the Atlantic and Pacific, and in the course of history
events fell that smashed beautiful things,
and the pieces were scattered throughout the earth
to make a reef of bones, and plates, and art.
The oceans weren't asleep after all when Beethoven

answered, writing down his booming message
to pulse and echo in the caverns of the past.
The earth turned red from Beethoven's imperfections,
which came to Mozart's perfect attention,
and Mozart fought back with a faultless rose.

Mozart's flawless signature spread across the sky
while Beethoven's was scrawled among the weeds,
and when Mozart held aloft his permanent rose
Beethoven coughed and tore through a spider's web,
and it was obvious, even to the distant tympani,
to the page-turners and the sorrowful oboe,
that music will murder the composer to gain its life,
and the light of music is silver encased in cement,
and the dark of music is missing under the lamp—
at which dead Mozart arrayed his bones in a skeleton,
and dead Beethoven spit and wrung an ear with one
        finger.

Ode to Night

A towel at 2 a.m., a damp throw rug by the bathtub,
suggests a life lived, a body cared for,
from which has run off the weight of a day
so that the towel is heavy with the hours, and the rug
carries an impression of footsteps
where someone has labored to finish a day refreshed.

Now faceless, timeless sleep
overtakes the rooms, the furnace exhales, but I
stay awake, a few words at a time,
an odd comma, an echo, a facsimile, a searching
reiteration of the inner shape
of a few small birds beneath night's eaves.

I cannot stop a sentence from fulfilling itself
any more than I can separate the helplessness of waking
from the nearly woken, or the dead
from the walking wounded. I am up late in wartime,
war's imprint within all of us who now
die of the earth and the water with which to wash it off.

Here at the threshold of the spirit,
not waking the body from soul, but bearing the day,
the weight that lay inside the very light
descends, even crumples, toward a day
without day and the endless nights of no night,
the prepossessing digestion of every inkling.

But enough of this. Better the memory of Moondog,
traipsing Times Square with his ethereal music
that would survive him in recordings,
and Joffre Stewart, anarchist of Chicago's South Side,
leafleting the streets, beaten by the police
who hit him where it wouldn't show.

Who's the kid on Rollerblades who trails the girls
on the Santa Monica boardwalk, half-strumming
a plastic electric guitar, wrapped in the sunshine
among the sporty, the fit and the successful,
his fluid line and talk a sweet, comic gesture
toward something, anything but living alone.

At what age does the life force turn,
and begin to give away its story, and the books, too,
and cease accumulating the material,
and the images, too, for a more abstract existence?
The towel has fallen from the rack,
my typing makes the birds rustle at the roofline,

and it was bedtime long ago.

Days of Superman

He can't help it about umbrellas, you'd think
they were rubberized splatters but to him are
spring-loaded popguns that shoot the rain.
This is childhood when an egg's so perfect,
so ideal, you have to crack it, and a milk bottle
is as full of feeling as mother's dress. He's a yarn
to relate of a rake and a leaf pile, of the circular
mysteries of a desk globe, how the Popsicle
man's wagon rang the day, and once a knife
sprang from its sheath and frightened the air.
He saw himself a coal, on its way to glass
or diamond, and his purple thumb his favorite
because the handsome hammer had chosen it.

Five to Seven

It's a dog straining at its leash
that sets the day
against the dawn, the new sun spotting
the sidewalk, and a slow ratcheting up
of machinery and a beehive of voices
picking up the pace of gossip, a humming of
harmonies, a layered chorus of order
and disorder, a knife blade shining briefly
in an alley, a car tire over the curb,
the siren, the clanging, the electric buzz,
now crisscrossing Times Square,
and the Staten Island Ferry spewing commuters
shaven or lipsticked from the bathrooms,
the mirror coated with steamy grimaces,
the workday rush to reach the rainbow
of a pension and a porch. Add in a bagel
with a schmear, some joe, a donut for ten,
and you've got America without a pennant,
a horde of faces without a flag,
up from the hole of night talk and beer,
ready to rumble in the subway, earplugs,
headphones, whatever it takes
to get back with a full shopping bag
emptied on the kitchen counter
while trying to cook and listen
to one person at a time.

Art Shoes

Let's turn a blind shoe to war. Let's point our shiny shoes
ahead and behind, to earth and sky, to time and no-time.
Let us kick up a rumpus to shake the maps.
We walked, we tapped, we scuffed. Now we stub our toes.
We laced up and stood on pointe when that was the
         point.
We looped, we arched, we coiled when circles were
         beauty.
We traced and retraced the steps from this to that.
We kept time to arrive at the timeless.
If the tongue could speak, the sole of a shoe cry out.
Listen! It says, "Walk, don't run." And then it says, "Run!"
It says life's a kick and a kicking, a stomp
of protest and pleasure. My own shoes, my everydays,
are wild to dance. They drag me foolish
to the music, they push and pull me to the beat.
They want to show me how free they are.
But they back up at the sound of boots.

An Apology to the Vietnamese and Iraqis

Fog and lamplight and a sleepless night
suggest a past to sit up with, in an armchair
with a book and a snack. A small boat putt-putts
somewhere under the cliff, passing the fennel
and ferns at waterside. I have screened out,
like you, the far away. For me, there's a khaki
sheen over Vietnam, and a sandstorm
will erase Iraq before the owl lifts its dinner
by the heel. That's the way we sleep now,
screening out the gunboats in the fog,
listening to the owl hunt farther and farther
to find his kill. Our nights are lampblack.

Bus Stop Essay on Rampant Capitalism

Property means money will own
our dust, the rinds of squeezed lemons,
soap film, and the reeds whistling in the swamp,
and they want the swans for themselves,
and the leftover thread from the tailor,
and the hair from the barbershop. They want fees
for dancing and a royalty for a quip. The rights
to Armageddon are still up for grabs. I was sitting
by a man who owned a coat in a storm
and was off his rocker, growling like an engine
uphill. He had a thrown-away half-hamburger
and a bag of wine. He was showing off his
best Fred Astaire, and he planned to visit
Hollywood and Cooperstown. He told me this
corner was his. He gave the breeze a cold shoulder
and his smell. He said he liked to find things.

Ordinary

I come often, it seems, to this café.
I don't have words to explain it,
but again I'm here. There's the woman
at the next table, the newspapers,
the blue pen left behind, and her coffee
is steaming the ceiling. Look how ordinary.
When I am dull, the ceiling is lower,
and the night sky is dull, stars or not,
and the sea with its repetitive swells
bringing what it brings in from the deep
to what we know of the shallows. I am,
myself, today, the shallows, a lone body,
lifeless find for a beachcomber on a break,
not so goofy as a geoduck but goofy
enough, and isn't "goofy" the word I need:
that sense of detached pleasure, nuances
of the life force, a nanophilosophy fit
to polish a sky, a ceiling or a window
until they are enough, which they were.

It

They had seen a red band roping the sun
and when that night they felt it
amidst a moaning from the leaves
and a fever
in the moonlight, they knew,
and they went to the woods and fell
to their knees, prepared to be taken
whole, extracted from among the non-
believers, to be among their kind,
and walk in golden slippers
to the point of no return.

Being Jewish, I was left behind,
not to be saved but to live with doubt
and suffering and the little
ecstasy one might be permitted
among the true religions, the Januses,
the fox-faced and intrepid,
for their Thine was the kingdom
and my Thine was the mud people
who could be loved only
if one could stop one's ears
against blasphemy,
since it was commonly known
Jesus wept on Sunday,
not on Saturday.

About His Eyes

It appears his eyes are half open, and I know why.
They think they are still in old Ukraine. They think
they are his father's eyes and, if the sea was too bright
to open them further, and if in steerage he didn't
want to see what was becoming of all of them,
and if when he opened one at a time in the New World
it seemed as if he were trying to focus or wanted
to ask a question, well, it was just that his Ukrainian
name sounds Armenian and he thinks he may already
have seen too much. He doesn't know how to smile,
but he laughs. He is someone I used to know well,
someone like me, someone like my father.

The Book of the Dead Man (Ghosts)

1. About the Dead Man and Ghosts

The dead man travels land, sea and sky to look for ghosts.

The dead man has seen them in the clouds, in smoke and
vapors, paling in fog, rising in the surf, dancing in
the flaring embers of campfires.

He has heard them shaking the bamboo, whistling in the
wind and the graveyard, flapping the roof shingles,
drumming on the walls, whipping the power lines
until they sing.

He has smelled the soap and softener of clean sheets.

He has tasted the residue of incense that appealed to
them.

He has felt the timbers shiver, the moonlight stutter and
the air cringe.

There was dread approaching, and it might have been the
ghost of history coming to extract payment.

There was weather in the air and the tent flaps slapping.

There was a drumming at a distance, or was it steps on
the stair?

The dead man's little pinky bone was still attached after
the campfire had been soaked and the scary tale
was over.

The dead man will not recover his mortal friends though
he welcome their spirit.

The dead man has seen ghosts appear to those who wish
to make peace with death.

He has sketched the human figure in the northern
  lights, in constellations, dust devils and
  waterspouts.
They appear in the distance.

2. More About the Dead Man and Ghosts

The dead man cheers for the Ghost Dance and all
  invocations of spirits.
The dead man has seen what his country did to its
  natives.
He knows that their spirits must rise up in the living.
He knows neither apparition nor daemon, neither the
  ethereal nor the incorporeal, neither the soul nor
  the specter shall turn back time.
Only the citizens have power who invoke the dead.
The dead man has counted the bodies of those who
  lived on ghostly in a cause.
He wants to believe the ghosts of Jefferson and Adams
  will overthrow the fascists.
For what good are ghosts who are pretty Pollys or skull
  bones, guilt-trippers, hand-slappers or buddies
  up from the egocentric psyche?
The dead man's ghosts have guts.
He hears them on the street corners speaking from the
  mouths of the rabid.
He sees them wrestling invisible opponents in doorways
  and alleys.
He waits for the day an army of ghosts lays waste to
  those who slaughtered the innocents.

The dead man will haunt America until it does right by
    its unseen.
Until then, or until the Earth meets the sun, he is not
    going anywhere.

Geezers

Bush, Cheney, Rumsfeld

It was a breeze to grow old.
The dust settled. Some dunes moved.
I left Long Island for the plains and mountains,
and here I am, a bit retired, a bit unstrung,
a little off my rocker still, but still first out
on the dance floor, as quick as ever to defend
the duck and the swan, the soft soap
if innocent, the quip if it zings a Yalie
or a social engineer. I am, like you, a witness
to the coffins that were Vietnam and Iraq,
to a political machine that came up three lemons.
Not every geezer is old, not every prez mature.
I am the big ears and the wide eyes
to whom time happened. I lived in stormy weather
writing songs of love because, tell me
if you know, who can help it?

Stubby Sag Harbor Sonnet

The petty interference with light occasioned by shade.
See the shade for what it is.
Sycamore that shadows my movements.
The locals drive to work by way of the water.
To make sure it is still there, a confirmation of their
      being.
Windows down, a sandwich at noon, a newspaper.
I have nothing to add to the nature of zero and one.
The click of a tiny chisel on jade once organized
      centuries.
Now we lack the silence that framed true words.
There will be stories lost to a roar of falling bricks.
There will be poems that swallowed hard.
They will use scorned prepositions and adjectives.
They will say nothing more than themselves.
They will return to the fold the fold's work.

The Book of the Dead Man
(Recent Dreams)

1. About the Dead Man's Recent Dreams

Call them ravaged castles in the air.
Think them fancy, fantasy, reverie or romance.
Dismiss them as head trips and chimeras.
He sees them day and night, call him a woolgatherer or
    stargazer.
He cannot stop his seeing what is not there.
Call it the prior future or the posthumous present.
For his sight when asleep is that of a brain loosed from
    the mind.
The dead man shuffled the deck, he crumpled the map,
    he trashed the tea leaves.
Now he must strain to hear the springy squeaking of life
    among the deciduous messages of fall.
Think him the fool, if you like, who speaks in riddles.
He has become the willful naïf, the one who closed his
    eyes to better see.
For now there is only the sea sweeping.
There are only the clues left gasping when the tide
    recedes.

2. More About the Dead Man's Recent Dreams

The dead man's dreams disappear in the light.
They make no promises, they are the body's dance, they
    are happenstance.
Who has ever died in his dreams and told?

He cannot see the face of the one whose hand reaches
for the door.
And have not many of his visions taken the bit and run
from view?
He has tried repeatedly to go to sleep in his dreams.
The dead man is not one to go flying while asleep, he is
grounded.
He has walked hot coals, lingered among auras, and
been taught if one says a thing three times it will
happen.
Wake up, he has said to himself, wake up, wake up.
He has blamed his dreams on the hour, on life, on a bite
of sweets.
He knows that dreams are not an effect but a cause.
Last night he spoke aloud the word "joker" but does not
know why.
He dreams of living forever for a few minutes at a time.

First-Generation American, Now the News

That his father had had to leave Ukraine
was the mystery that penetrated a world view
before he had one. He could see in the pebbles,
in the gravel sidewalk, the fragility of location.
The sky seemed lower on school days. The war
was radio then, the pictures it made in his mind
something like a dramatic storm, the cannons
muffled in dark clouds, a bolt now and then
rifling toward ground. Those who had once landed
on Iwo Jima wore no medals and told no stories.

Now the storm in the mind that covered world events
has come to earth, and up from the earth.
Tsunami and flood roughen the mind. What smooth
talk or thought rivals the revelations of force?
Those who lose homes or lives elsewhere
are proof of the absurd. You want philosophy?
I'm here, dry, plenty to eat and drink. I came here
by dumb luck. I have a little money to give away.
They say you can grow up to be anything.
I wanted to do more than survive. More than love.

Yes

We need to think of what might grow in the field
from our ashes, from the rot of our remains,
from tillage and spoilage, from the watery corn
plowed under. We need to picture lilies of the valley
and the hard weeds on the mountain haloed by clouds,
and the minutest beads of water as they roll up
into raindrops to replenish what we relinquished
through expiration. We have been breathing-in
the wild rosebuds and the spoor left by those who
avoid us, we have been to the sea and the forest
to learn who we are, and it is time to say yes
to the intangible reach of our being, the stirring
that sifts, pans and rearranges the billion parts
of us, who once thought we were goners.

"Astronomers May Have Reason for Milky Way's 'Lumpiness'"

USA Today, January 9, 2006

They know now why we are reeling in space,
the sun a swinging lamp in a warped galaxy. Brother,
what new ritual will emerge from this knowledge
blistering sinners on the corner, its lungs bellowing
as it hands us a leaflet? There's a lump in the breast
of the muse, who once had a lump in her throat,
to see the moon handled like a marble, and Earth
like ground teeth, bones and powder. Let me hear
again the sea hammering and feel the new sheet
cool as she slides into bed beside me. Let the desk
smell of fresh ink and the lawn of cut grass,
and above all let the news of the day be more
and more of the unattainable so I can reach all
I want and still my arms will be around her.

Regardless

We are only the breeze in a dancer's skirt,
an explosion of dust, a face in the soapstone,
a rustle among weeds, the squeak
of a rocker where the old ones strung out
their years in story. It's mashed potatoes
and a gravy boat. It's goosebumps seeing
a lemony lion in *The Peaceable Kingdom*
or your curled lips popping to keep time
with Parker at Birdland. A storm can travel
inland, shaving the dunes and undoing
the equipoise between events. If this is to be
a swan song, let it be plain vanilla
engineered so richly it fills you. One man's
dune is another's desert, a good read
is another's mouth washed out with soap.

West Coast Oceanic

Time whitened the shell of van Gogh's ear.
It bleached the nautilus left by the tide
and spidered the backs of my hands. Now goliaths
roam the earth who were ants, and raindrops
wallop the land. Plaster turns into mud and, if
we run, we run till the end of time. The foliage
makes it slow going, the ice is slippery, the water
does not part. Let them preach of the past
full of myth, when it was sufficient that a story
not be disproved. The sun is my pilot light,
I shall not want it to fail or the moon to cease turning
its white blade through the clouds. I saw in the dawn
a plate in a chromium sky and, if it was only
light lifting the dew, still the surf was already saying,
"Be reckless." A dozen surfers have paddled out
to listen for a thunderclap inside a breaker
that won't yet have happened, and mount it,
and ride it away from the sunset. I watch from the pier
with distracted nonchalance, and the sea filling
my lungs. I want what everyone wants: more.

Veterans of the Seventies

His army jacket bore the white rectangle
of one who has torn off his name. He sat mute
at the round table where the trip-wire veterans
ate breakfast. They were foxhole buddies
who went stateside without leaving the war.
They had the look of men who held their breath
and now their tongues. What is to say
beyond that said by the fathers who bent lower
and lower as the war went on, spines curving
toward the ground on which sons sat sandbagged
with ammo belts enough to make fine lace
of enemy flesh and blood. Now these who survived,
who got back in cargo planes emptied at the front,
lived hiddenly in the woods behind fence wires
strung through tin cans. Better an alarm
than the constant nightmare of something moving
on its belly to make your skin crawl
with the sensory memory of foxhole living.

Oppression

I begin by a window, a lamp over my shoulder,
and a glance outside to see
if a light snow is falling or if it's just the day's
floaters in an old man's eyes. I check the clouds
for signals and cuneiforms
among the pillows, and the mountain ash
for its resistance to autumn, and only then
am I ready for the news, the artillery,
the detonators, the beheadings,
the blood stains and marrow, the numbers,
and the black hearts of the officials. I need
the proof Peary sought in ice, and Odysseus
at sea, to believe a fox, say, or a cougar
can get away, and men and women also,
so camouflaged in plain view that we see them
only in the representations, in the stories
or briefly visible in the leaves or sky,
escapees surviving by feel or ducked down
in their thoughts, unable to speak freely.

The Time I Tore My Kneecaps Off (*La La*)

I have a place inside me sticky with old cartilage.
If you lean in, you can hear the tendons squeak,
and feel a smoky tickle in your nose like that
of a just-extinguished match. There is dust there,
too, and minute shards of bone that pricked
the surgeon's finger. He was the one in the light,
while I was blind. I saw his glasses flash
as the light went out, and something—a curtain?—
rattled and rustled. I woke with a taste
like dry sand, lips swollen, thankful for ice chips.
By the time I quit the ward, I was nearly nuts
from the swish of the mop in the hallway
and the thin milk at meals. For the next four months,
I lived in a bed at home and laughed about it.

Weapons of Mass Destruction

to the memory of Asa Baber

Like all armies, we were sent to mop up
the political fallout, but found only dust, empty milk
     cans,
burlap bags of nuts, and pools of wax:
residue of the blind embargo that shut off the lights.
From our leader's angle, they were no more worthy
than the yellow bellies of Vietnam, for these warriors
swung the same sword that had been defeated
by that fly in the soup, Ho Chi Minh. Moss and lichen
cover the graves. The memorial in the capital
holds out an obsidian wall of casualties to their relatives,
and the relatives keep coming, wrenched with loss,
muffling their cries as they trace the names. Asa said
not all the names are etched there, having died
beyond the boundaries of the war. Today, I marry
          Vietnam
to Iraq, I see where they match, I see how hard it is
to quit now, for we are like a bird with one wing,
helpless on the flaming sand, should fish or star
explode, the comet come that we always knew was there.

Why

One Sunday, when the famous thorns have pierced
the fingers of lovers the world over who took roses
to their desire, when the professors have gone dumb,
faced with the amorous, blinded by each ecstatic
escape from time, by love and art, and the land,
and the minister hesitates before the approving
congregation, a helpful cloud bank will appear
to block the sun, the Saturday revelers will awake
in a chill, unable to recall what or why, and the sight
of a peignoir will have lost its titillation. I have to
make up a future without the aid of a rabbi or priest,
who have enough to do without the threat of
forgiveness and a cloud to stand on saying thanks
for eternity. I love you today. I'm not waiting
for the weekend or the right time. None of this is
about me or us. The world is full of broken wings,
where pigeons roost outside the church window
cooing, or is it clucking, twitching to spot peace.

The Book of the Dead Man (Time)

1. About the Dead Man and Time

When the dead man rises from bed, time smiles.

Time itself snickers at the dead man rising from bed.

The chortling sounds in bells and buzzers, radio
whispers, sunshine fizzing in the leaves, the
wheat and corn rustling from near and far, the
ten thousand things to be remembered.

The clock face laughs at his ache to be active, as the
moon laughs at his lethargy, his ennui, his apathy,
his teetering between means and ends.

The dead man is the liquid that stained the antique
veneer.

He is private.

He has a hammer in his ear, a pin in his knee, and a
knot in his groin.

He is a rake passé and a married man.

The dead man offers time . . . more time.

He hath washed the lamb and the linen and ironed the
work shirt.

The dead man, dead and alive, is an instrument of war
and of peace.

Neither cotton in his ears nor a turn of the knob can
stop the mental pictures he makes from the
evening news.

In the control room, a stopwatch measures the bones to
be unearthed, the depth at which a soldier sticks
in sand, the several times the field cook turns the
ladle to serve the troops hot meals.

The dead man thinks time is not the measure of time.
Bodies are a measure of time, the smell of loess is a
      measure of time, the taste of roots, the feel of
      the shrunken and putrid, a whistle fading as the
      mourners walk from the gravesite, the moon
      circling is a measure of time.
The dead man and his counterpart are a pair.
They have looked up from the lowland and down from
      the bluff, they have slept on a rug and a bench,
      they have slumbered in a box in the framework
      of time.
The dead man has time on his side and time in his
      pocket.
He has had a taste of time, and he likes it as much as
      cake or a pear.
The dead man lives equally in Newtonian time and
      Einsteinian time.
As the world hurries to convert uranium, the dead man
      feels for time's edge.

2. More About the Dead Man and Time

The dead man did not plan to teeter between life and
      death, here and there, or now and then, it just
      happened.
It was not his doing when the cotton shirt wrinkled for
      good and the instruments could no longer be
      tuned, it was time.
It was time that turned the big ladle in the sky.

It was time that wore out the rug to show who had
        come and gone, it was time loosened the bed
        frame so love creaked.
The dead man does not believe in time but sticks to the
        subject.
He does not believe in time but in the time it takes.
For in time the sun will fizzle, and the bone, potsherd
        and tooth unearthed by the archaeologist's rake
        are the records of time.
Who knows time better than the dead man?
The dead man knows that time is the other face of no-
        time, the backside of an alarm clock, the knob
        turned to Off that controlled the fatal gas.
Time that stopped for Houdini is more than magic for
        the dead man.
Time is the unseen liquid that oils the edge of the earth.
Time is the invisible pin that fixes the moon above.
Oh, time in a box, time on the head of the nail before
        the hammer strikes, time that takes the silkworm
        by surprise, time that bluffs at night, time that
        washes the wheat.
Time that releases the sound of the cowbells, time of
        the time clock at the end of the workday.
The dead man does not applaud time, but what men
        tell of it.
Under the veneer of time, life and death pair up to iron
        out their differences.
The dead man knows he alone cannot stop the
        stopwatch.

Bent

Trying to fix a corkscrew that exploded
when it popped from my hand, I am
distracted for a moment from the signs
of age that signal to me in the form of
spaces where there ought to be memories
and words where there ought to be
other words. Lying on the grass to shape
a narrative in the clouds, there was a time
my head seemed to be there, my thoughts
rose into the cumulus and were carried—
indeed, swaddled—smoothly from past
to future, from first horizon to night's arch.
These clouds today have snow in mind
but cannot let go. I poke at them, press
them to fulfill the season, but they slip away.
When Stieglitz photographed the clouds,
he captured his emotions, equivalents. He
was young then and the sky could still
exhaust him. There is a highway going west
where more than not a radiant sun slivers
a portal in an amber sky. No one ever
believes it is God. It is one thread among
the many that will net the colors of a sunset
farther down the road. There time retreats
beneath one's wheels, and the plot's afoot.

About the Author

Now seventy and retired after forty years on the faculty of the Iowa Writers' Workshop, Marvin Bell is known for his poetic independence, visible in eighteen previous books, his accessibility to all areas of the reading and writing community, and his no-nonsense teaching. He is the creator of a form known as the dead man poem, for which he is both famous and infamous. He and his wife, Dorothy, live in Iowa City, Iowa, and Port Townsend, Washington.

The Chinese character for poetry is made up of two parts: "word" and "temple." It also serves as pressmark for Copper Canyon Press.

Since 1972, Copper Canyon Press has fostered the work of emerging, established, and world-renowned poets for an expanding audience. The Press thrives with the generous patronage of readers, writers, booksellers, librarians, teachers, students, and funders—everyone who shares the belief that poetry is vital to language and living.

Major funding has been provided by:

Anonymous
The Paul G. Allen Family Foundation
Lannan Foundation
National Endowment for the Arts
Washington State Arts Commission

For information and catalogs:

COPPER CANYON PRESS
Post Office Box 271
Port Townsend, Washington 98368
360-385-4925
www.coppercanyonpress.org